Hugo Claus

Even Now

POEMS

Selected and translated from the Dutch by David Colmer

archipelago books

Selected and translated from *Gedichten 1948–2004* by Hugo Claus
published by Uitgeverij De Bezige Bij, Amsterdam

Archipelago Books
232 3rd Street #A111
Brooklyn, NY 11215
www.archipelagobooks.org

Library of Congress Cataloging-in-Publication Data
Claus, Hugo, 1929–2008.
[Poems. Selections. English]
Even Now : poems / Hugo Claus ; selected and translated
from the Dutch by David Colmer.
First Archipelago Books edition.
Text is in English.
"Selected and translated from *Gedichten 1948–2004* by Hugo Claus"
ISBN 978-1-935744-88-7
I. Colmer, David, 1960– II. Title.
PT6410.C553A2 2013
839.31'164–dc23   2013010326

Cover art: Hugo Claus and Corneille

Archipelago gratefully acknowledges the generous support
from Lannan Foundation, the Flemish Literature Fund,
the National Endowment for the Arts,
and the New York State Council on the Arts, a state agency.

Printed in the United States of America

Contents

from **Sonnets**

from **The Traces**

from **Cruel Happiness**

from **In Case of Emergency**

Even Now

POEMS

from **Registration** [1948]

For the Poet Antonin Artaud

Among us, the strays, the strangers,
the ones who never landed, the deranged,
a pale captain has died.

I see the arteries in his temples
no longer throbbing.
His face, a carved paving stone,
has finally stopped moving.

That we are scarred for life
is clear to them, the balanced souls,
the undisturbed characters,
in all their level hours.

They broke his fragile back.
They locked him up with a chair and bread and straw.
They called him mad and sick.
They pitied him.

I will meet him still
under bridges, in the empty train station.
He will put his arm around my shoulder.
Towards morning he starts drilling,
shaking my fibres,
until I scream, Artaud, Artaud.

I see the arteries in his temples
no longer throbbing.

Break the belt of impotence.
Crack the shell of infertility.
My dead greyhound, my ravaged tower,
my bleeding, stillborn,
burnt-out man, Antonin Artaud.

from **Without Due Process** [1950]

I.

We've known it now for centuries,
that the moon is dangling by a thread
attached to heaven, hell or nothing at all.
That the thick blue paint of night
is drooping down into the streets
to wrap around you like a deep blue robe
this evening when you head for home,
dawdling ne'er-do-wells, theatre and recital-goers,
nighthawks, people who are alive,
and that the night will soon be washed away
like cheap blue ink from years ago
and afterwards the pale, pink skin
of heaven, hell or nothing at all
will shine through and no longer pale,
especially not the pink nothing like a girl's
soft and salty sex,
and afterwards heaven and hell and nothing at all
will dry out, go mouldy and decay,
just as old loves and bad habits,
doses of the clap, faithful pieces of furniture
and bunkers from pre-1914 must die,
with no one's help, in a corner, on a sandstone slab,
like cunning old crabs must die.

III.

In autumn and in wet winters
there are days when nothing happens
in the house. Nothing except breaking the past,
like breaking a day that's passed in glass,
like melting chunks of pond ice,
so that its number's up, the past's, its number is up.
But the past and today just won't lie down,
they turn circles on a carousel, joining hands,
becoming weeks again and months and finally seasons.
There are days
that the clocks of every tower in the land
run half an hour slow
and not one of those winter people notices,
and the lost half hours, saved by no one,
ride through villages and towns, unseen, behind trams
and horse-drawn carts and clump together to form a day,
the way that snow makes a man of ice,
a day of ice for the lonely,
for whom every night is holy
like tonight.

from **The Joyous and
Unforeseen Week** [1950]

I

It can rain and it can blow,
but the magpie still speaks on Sunday,
the day of dogs and the blind.

Oh, Sun-sham-day.

To the wooden priest in his box
I whisper, For me, defused, deactivated,
                    deadened, despairing,
              this day is no valid reason.

4

Beside the water where the grass grows
like the hair of dead women
the girls lie on Friday nights,
surprising passers-by with a glimpse
of thighs in stockings with a sailor
in between.

Unshakeable confidence
steals up on you then, oh, Freya-day stroller,
you wide-branching bridegroom.

from **Bounds** [1955]

Home

Father was eating partridge and Mother wasn't there
and me and Joris were talking murder
and fleeing and which trains to take
when the sun rolled into the loft
and lay there shining in the hay.
Father cursed and said, God sees me.
Joris fled
and I kept playing with the trains
which ran across the floor
on electricity.

from **A House Between
Night and Morning** [1953]

Exercises

7

Tonight, the whatever of May, at nine p.m.,
On the dirt road past the young and rustling corn,
In the froth of the summer rain,
I was misfortunate enough to think of you.

I thought:
If you're gone, if you desert,
If you want to be dead to me,
If you want to cower in the brothel of forgetfulness
With your arms over your head,
If you want to walk off unnoticed from one day into the next,
If you want to play with memory's pearls,
Tying memory around your neck like a wreath.

I thought:
Where will be the grace in life's bird cry,
Where will be the grace in day after day of
Swollen sickening time?

Gistel By Bruges

Village of cows and willows,
Church tower and rhododendrons in rows.

In a curtain of rain
In a fold of the sky and in the light,
The bronze mayor sits on a bronze box.

Moss from the palm of your hand,
Rain from the whites of your eyes,
Hedge tops from your lashes,
Hills of ochre from your breast,
And the folds of the whole country from your body.

And the ringed bulls bellow
Through the circle of hay to the open fields,
But the nearby cows don't make a sound.

A Rendezvous

Again you say, Bye and Goodnight,
Words that come at me with the crooked gait
Of the tortoise in the kitchen.
The fourteen monkeys in the garden
Cower under the rhubarb leaves,
Huddling together to weep in the rain.

The wire that clangs against the smoke-stained walls
When the wind gets up.
The last cigarette. The smoke. The ash.
We have got 30 years left to live
And then centuries.

The lift starts up. The footsteps in the hall.
I tremble briefly. You're caged in now
And won't get past me again.

I Write You Down

My woman, my pagan altar,
Which I caress and play with fingers of light,
My young wood, my wintering place,
My tender, unchaste, neurasthenic sign,
I write your breath and body down
On lined music paper.

And in your ear I promise brand-new horoscopes,
Preparing you again for trips around the world
And a stay somewhere up on an alp.

But with gods and constellations,
Eternal happiness can grow deathly tired,
And I have no home, I have no bed,
Not even flowers for your birthday.

I write you down on paper
While you swell and bloom like an orchard in July.

Behind Bars

Saturday Sunday Monday sluggish week and weakened days

A still-life a landscape a portrait

A woman's brows
Closing as I approach

The landscape with blond calves wading a river
Where the season of compassion is burnt
Into the Prussian blue of the fields

Then I painted another still-life
With unrecognisable brows and a mouth like a moon
With a spiral like a trumpet of redemption
In the Jerusalem of my room.

An Angry Man

No house too black
For me to live in

No morning too bright
For me to wake up in
As in a bed

That's how I live and watch in this house
Between night and morning

Walking on fields of nerves
And digging my nails into every
Uncomplaining body that approaches

Saying chaste words like
Rain and wind apple and bread
Dark and viscous blood of women

Caligula

Where later radishes and mignonette will flower
In May that is
In a garden by the tracks of a country train
The wind
Is freezing now in December
And in that wind without light without shepherds without birds
Without any chance at all a foal has frozen to death

I've brought it here and put it under glass
I gaze away the days and hours
(That pass me by on the wide path
Of this existence which reasonably
We tread in sin with no great deeds)
And wait until thankful and thawed
The foal looks up and speaks its first word.

from **Tancredo Infrasonic** [1952]

Las Hurdes

We know neither bread nor meat
We sleep on leaves that turn to compost for our stony land

Our houses have no windows
And in our village there are 14 dwarves and 30 idiots

It rains and our levees leak
It doesn't rain We pray and our earth stays dry
Like our skin
Like our throats that swell and crack

He who is our father is our lover
And our mothers die young

Shame is our portion
Disgrace our daily meal
Our faces are rank with weeds

We look into your camera We are real
And you are right to say, "They are Las Hurdes."

West Flanders

A gaunt song a dark thread
Land like a sheet
That sinks

Springtime land of milk and farms
Willow-wood children

Feverish summer land when the sun
Spawns its young in the corn

Golden enclosure
With the deaf-and-dumb farmers at their dead hearths
Praying to God to "forgive us
His trespasses against us"

With the fisherman burning in their boats
With the mottled animals the frothing women
Who sink

Land I dawn in you My eyes are shards
I am in Ithaca with holes in my skin
I borrow your air when I speak
Your bushes and lindens concealed in my words

My letters are West Flanders: dune and polder

I drown in you
Land you are a gong in my skull and at times
Later in ports
A conch: May and beetle Dark bright
Earth.

Bye

A morning like always your house is empty
We count and one by one the days
Step into the cage

One sees I see you see
The hidden animals in the cool mirror see
This keeps it buried

The knife that rusts the blood that clots
The bricks porous the milk sour

One says you say
With a blinded voice a frozen gesture

Bye
Bye dear children bye.

from **The Oostakker Poems** [1955]

Bitter tastes

Bitter tastes the herb of memory.

Artillery, chunks of phosphorus,
Chalky stubble turnips surround the house and who
Is not watching there, unchaste sentinels waiting for the sign
Of the burning bush, of the horn,
Of the helmeted weathercock of hate?

One step and monkeys start swinging, slithering,
Sliding in on fingers,
Forcing entry into my resting blood. Living there swiftly,
Living there slowly. Until it burns in the hay of all words,
Until it burns in the bygone field, the drowned days and
Their fermenting corn.

The Singer

The singer is not free
But fast and scornful and skimming the peaks like a pond.

He is not free because his transfixed cascade
And worm-eaten wood resound in his throat, tongue and mouth.
Let loose in his skin, this house,
The singer greets neither cuckoo nor bird catcher

Nor the furtive watchers in the low country.

The singer is his song.

The Mother

There is no me, no me but in your earth.
When you cried out your skin shivered
And my bones caught fire.

(My mother, imprisoned in her skin,
Changes by the measure of the years.

Her eyes are pale, escaped from the urging
Of the years by looking at me and calling me
Her joyful son.

She was no bed of stone, no feverish beast,
Her joints were a litter of kittens,

But my skin stays unforgivable to her,
The crickets in my voice unmoving.

"You have outgrown me," she says slowly,
Washing my father's feet, then falling silent
Like a woman without a mouth.)

When your skin cried out my bones caught fire.
You laid me down, I can never bear this image again,
I was the welcome but murderous guest.

And now, in manhood, I am a stranger to you.
You see me approaching and you think, "He is
The summer, he shapes my flesh and keeps
The dogs in me alert."

While you die on your feet every day, not with me,
Apart, there is no me, no me but in your earth.
Turning inside of me, your life is lost, you won't
Come back to me, I cannot recover from you.

A Father

Dancing or defeated,
Imprisoned in human warmth, we are already slowing
In the thickets of disinclination, in the contaminated fields,
Following on the heels of the mutilated, who whisper.
Their lips dry in the sun, the late sun.

We hear the dusk, we hear
The daily rattle from the scaffold,
We hear the flayed cub, we hear
The Jew burning in the bush and the crippled nun,
The judge's sisters, god-fearing and voluptuous,
The heathens in the park, the raven shooters and the crusaders.
We hear them all.

A beak eats out of our mouths.
A tropic encircles our blood.

And under the linden, dewy in its shade,
The father lies for days, days on end, unswayable,
Watching his worn-down children.

A Virgin

Between clouds and royal ferns
The mares will ride tonight in the white field
Growing whiter.

Between thorns and rhododendrons the farmers beat
The children who came too soon.

And where the black iron maiden
Subdues me
The tower shudders, the holy signs tremble.

Listen:
"I am the fatal mother, desire me,
implore me, awaken in my sun—I
Will be with you till your breath fails."

Listen: "You will not heal but live
On the edge of my life.
In sand, you will acknowledge me."

In a harbour
That breathes like a woman,
Not restlessly but endlessly,
Her body flutters,
And where she swells all buttons snap,
All skins peel.

Where she swells I surrender, foundering in her bucking
Boats, her rising triumph,
Her sinking, slackening, sailing inland sea.

A Woman

I

Hair roaring with laughter,
Seagull eyes, a pouch on her belly,
A mother or another traitor,
Who knows this scorching woman?

Her nails come close to my wood,
Her tainted claws awaken my skin,
She blares in my hair like a hunting horn.

She approaches in pleats and bolts,
In heat, in resin, in splashing,
While I, in a state of desire,
Extended like a rifle and
Ready to engage and kill,
Enclose, plough and fell,
Bending, kneeling, the heady animal
Between her leather-soft knees.

She splits my skittle
In the familiar warmth.

5

The husky night and the cart
Of time that drives into the night,
Rattling.

Your hair, the seagull nest.
The meerschaum hills in which,
Toothed, the fruit that splits.

The lizards, the stone woodpeckers
Swaying in the leaves,
In the furious leaves.

Hear the hooves of the horse Desire
Fleeing down the road.
Hear in the fields the moorcock, the hare,
The chattering teeth of love.

12

Her mouth: the tiger, the leap, the spinning top
Round and round to seven months of summer.
Her body: liana waiting to ignite.
A shell of wheat.

Flat is my white,
As white as a fish of stone.
I have been razed to the skin.
My population purged.

She has become someone else. Strange to my eye,
The one who lived in the scruff of my neck.

The Catchword: House

3

One leap
And I dived
Blind
Into the arms of a wind so bitter
The land let go its hold and I
Was impregnated by winter
And winter was the fury
Of my coagulating skin.

Darkness
Visited me
The blood
Of women asked and swiftly climbed and leapt
Into my backbone. And I became flesh and claw
And branch. Brittle
With desire I grew, a
Rider of the night-time

Strangers
Who I,
The animal,
Could no longer escape. In this season
Strangers
Are my life. Turning, they collapse,
As hot as women in the snow.

8

The night blows and beats its mutilated wings.
Rising from the uncertain earth the broken branch
Pierces my body.

Winter ends again and
No-one is mine.

From the avaricious woods,
The avaricious rats come riding through the grass.

12

Loneliness is a home.
(A home closes—warm

Lives a season in lodgings and
Becomes a face—soft

Is loneliness and ripens thought-
Fully from child to man and corpse.)

Don't be like a home.
Love is a cramp and

(A murder) reaching for the
Moment: a dying executioner, a splitting conch.

Mirrors ripen. Don't be like a mirror.

from **A Painted Rider** [1961]

N.Y.

Over the rippled asphalt, through the steam
billowing from the grates,
three Black warriors carry a pink summer evening gown
like a senator's wife.

On the concrete peninsula, in the bronze palaces
—drip trays for the growling jets above—
everybody buys the thinking man's cigarette,
everybody chews their ground beef with nickel-plated teeth,
everybody washes in film-star milk.

What protects me from
this cannon fever?

A design around my left nipple
eloquently executed by Tattoo Joe,
the electric Rembrandt.

Chicago

Under the crossword of concrete beams,

between the peroxide bitches
and the gastric ulcer advertisements,

besieged by the bells of salvation's armies
contaminated by soot and sugar
and humiliated by insulted Negroes,
a greyer desire awakens
in every desire.

And whiter gentlemen greet me,
a stranger in their nest,
a friend and fellow pest.

There is reason here to hang,
reason enough, no one gives a dang
between forgetting and release.

A verse from Luke won't help you here,
nor a leather dragon on your back
nor chewing on the almond herb.

I'll be replaced here soon
by a mouth full of grit.

Travelling

For nine days the lost donkey stood up to the buzzards,
now its remains are reeking on the roadside.

The sun, a stag that wants to catch the stars, those vultures,
doesn't touch the riders,
begging by the wheels.

Girls who keep house in wooden boxes
make offerings to Jesus and Zapata.

On the way from Puerto Marqués to Oaxaca
I throw three hundred and eighty butts at wizened old men.

Uxmal

On the river sometimes when the strange weather
bursts into flame
a skeleton will sometimes creak
like a piece of furniture or a badly healed jaw.
This is what the natives hear. Unmoving.
Expressing no desires,
They ask no questions quickly shutting off, close-lipped,
they live in singular devastation.

Above the anthracite fields where Mayas
played ballgames in front of the House of the Dwarf
a vulture flicks its wing and swoops down on an anteater in the grass.
This is what we hear. And take photos of the prey.
Later we descend backwards from the Rain God's altar
to avoid offending his eyes
and land in nettles.
(For the ladies every niche is dripping with phallic significance.)
We live in multiple bedazzlement.

She

I

Two horses in the hay, a grey and one with a blaze,
tied together and stamping,

a winter's tale about that,
my memory of us already
homework for later days.

The contagion that transforms me
(a would-be hero becomes a shepherd
racing flames across the field)
distorts our gestures, animals and clouds.

In rooms I hear myself ask about before
and in the role of croaking judge
I speak of our old arbitrary horses
law and cancer.

2

Even if for you and me the world
has long been a domain of prickles and sponges,
we still ride down avenues.

Cured of stars but not yet addicted
to the manifold silence
we warm ourselves on the simple weather

and play in the hairy year
as if jumping at branches full of apples.
Playing, but dozens of horse flies from outside bite
and snitches from somewhere else cut me down to size.
"Look, a kite," you say
and I see you burnt by phosphorus.
"Look, a beetle," you say
and I see you crushed by a tank.

And beyond this, I sometimes think, you betray my voice,
but speaking without you is a plea to a mirror,
fleeing into the worst kind of wood.

Often you *are* my voice, you,
a trap for hare's tails, a cuckoo's egg,
you, my bed.

6

Sometimes, outside of your presence,
I want to slide silence into the tipping day,
delaying the dissipation.

But outside muddled circles
the dancer does not live.

In every room your fussing lies in wait
in every breath your hooks still try their luck
and you chatter away, my marsupial,
yes, you, who conjugates my misery
as sweetly as the verb to fuck.

Sleep tight tonight, milady,
and eat your dreams raw.
Tomorrow my marrowbones will be ready again
for your miraculous mouths.

The Sphinx Speaks

You there on three legs, night is falling in the peaks,
an abyss is looming ahead
and will end your bitter drivel.

Seagulls still blow through your life,
but your shins are chalky
and your sowing is done.

No lamp in this debris, no watcher on the cliffs
where you shrink. For all that the taste
of almond still shakes you up,
as much as you're an ape in your delusions,

you here on three legs, give up the fight
and say goodnight to your children.
A seagull is already skimming the sea
to catch you up with salt and sand.

The Panama Canal

When the news came—no news came.

We drilled to the stream's grave and carved
through the hyacinths that smothered its bed

when the news came.

And the news, translated and suppressed, pierced our chests
and broke the already motionless rock in our crotch.

It was a judgement on our customs,
a white law, scarcely explained:

"No more fumes, no pipes, no powders or herbs,
no sniffing or sucking the life-giving grass."

Then we sat down and became the slush
in the sludge of the dredging machines.

With transplanted brains, banished to the blood-sapping cold,
we sat down by the foreign sea.

Strangled our parents with their queues, hung our children
in a bunch from the crane

and waited under the buzzards for the surging tide
to catch us in its cloud-sown waves.

Message to the Population [1962]

(an appeal in an extremely free verse form, delivered at Amsterdam's Krasnapolsky Hotel on 1 January 1962, and dedicated to two of those present: Remco Campert and Simon Vinkenoog)

My very dear friends,
Sometimes I tell a story (as one might expect of a poet)
About the winter which, in the white night,
Sends a flock of seagulls over the besieged city.
And then you nod, "Right, that's a poet talking."

And if in a romance I wish to record
The lamentations of the people in their gardens
You whisper, "Sure."
Because I say so, because I am a poet.

But if I say, "Soon a gigantic wind will blow over you all,
A gruesome wind from God
And nothing will be left of any of you,"
Then you splutter and say, "He is a poet."
(I.e., he should concern himself with books and broads,
but not with the delicate, fundamental, incalculable
cogs and wheels of politics and the intricate swinging system
of left and right, for and against, red or dead.)

My very dear friends,
On this winter's day, the first of the year 1962,
There is much that I love, including, for example,
My wife, my three brothers, my father and my mother,
And there is much that I abhor, including, for example,
Those who have a lot of money when I have too little,
Writers who write badly and women without necks.
Well, of what I cherish and what I hate,
There will soon, after that wind, be nothing left.

Friends, God came to me and said,
"Claus, I made you out of nothing, what do you think of that?"
And I said, "Thank you very much, God."

And he said, "And to nothing you will return. Huh?"
And I said, "Thank you very much, God. Just say the word."
But then a man came up to me and said,
"I'd rather be dead than red,
And if I want to die then so do you.
I'd rather be one hundred per cent dead than just a little bit red.
All hands on deck, our ship will never sink.
None of us will ever be even a little bit pink!"
And I said, "Thanks a lot, man, but I pass."
And he said, "Wars ennoble when they are noble wars,
fought for freedom's holy cause."
Then I said, "Thanks a lot, man, but I pass,
Because what's going to come is no war
But a single gruesome, obscene wind from your God
And after that, nothing else."
And I said, "I don't want to see your God's arse."

Nothing else after that? Will all our eyeless
Toothless, chickenless grandchildren slough off
Their blistered skin down to the sixteenth toe?
Where in the blackest night does a blind man see a lighter black?
I hope that the gentlemen*
Will be able to explain that to you shortly.
I already know it all too well (I am a poet)
And it sickens me to realise
How I am making a fool of myself.
Because how can I make a fist?
One officer with a regulation truncheon
Would take care of the brainwork in my head in a jiffy.
Let alone: 3 police officers and 2,000 soldiers. Let alone the
Millions who would rather be red than dead.

*At Krasnapolsky, the speakers after Claus were the clergyman Kater, the biologist Van der
Lek, the teacher H. Herbers and councillor Van der Sluis-Fintelman.

There's nothing to be done about it, so I do nothing
Except say these words, which also do nothing,
To you who also do nothing.
Admit it, it's insane.
Because anyone who's not spent and bent from hope and despair
Isn't sitting here
But waiting in their warm house with coffee and cake
And calculating which corner of the cellar
Is best for the construction of a better, double, crossways cellar,
For later. When the wind comes.

My very dear friends,
When that wind descends over you tomorrow
And you are taken up in Gods' fart
What good will hope and despair do you?
Let us head homewards,
Because don't you see how paltry brittle fragile
This peace is,
When someone like me argues about it
And someone like you and you and you and you
With spent bent words and nicely flammable
Banners and books.
That is why, dear friends, there will be
No message from me on the first day of the year,

But *an announcement for the population.*

This is the announcement.
Go home. Later on television there will be
The Tales of Hoffmann, Eurovision.
Watch it.
Afterwards, once you have digested your evening meal
And your thought processes are a little slower,

Sit down in front of your mirror,
Pull out your breadknife,
Hold it against your throat, and recite
The prayer of those who order and rule your days,
The prayer of your governments on earth,
Who are the bowels of God.

Our Father
Who art in Heaven
Blessed be Thy Bomb
Your Kingdom come
Your Megatons ignite here on earth
As they do in Heaven.
Give us this day our nuclear weapons
And forgive us our provisional peace
As we forgive those who annoy us by moaning for peace.
And lead us not into the temptation of disarmament
That we may incinerate and disappear
For ever and ever
Amen.

from **Peripheral Poems to**
L'Inferno, **Canto XIII** [1962]

I.

Where are you going? Why? Hollow questions, these,
and perfectly suited to fathers and judges!
We danced around their questions, spinning, swish, swish,
we, perfectly vacuous, we, ornate dolls.

"Just don't get us pregnant!" the girlies screeched
and the menfolk held back meekly
between a squeal and a bounce, and a pounce.
Oh no, nowhere on earth
did we feel more at home
than under the maddest of skirts.

But God sent down a surly aviator
to sprinkle his ingredients among us:
virtues, wrinkles, solitude.
The nights grew older and longer.
And then, without a sign or word, a grumbling verdict
was passed. That's right! Justice could be done!

How else can we explain that we
unnecessarily, improbably, unjustly,
were dancing slowly by the sea?

Now often, when the evening falls like snow,
a thing or creature moves towards us. And it
reaches us and in our pity-hollowed trunks,
it bears its fatal young.

from **An Eye for an Eye** [1963]

(after the ancients)

1 Him

My soul says, Run,
even if it costs you money and love
So says my soul
But I don't move an inch, I can't
Because my soul, the snake, is still mad about that little
black-haired bitch!

2   Her

An evening like any other. Nothing
to tell me you were present in the world.
I received no notification

I could have missed you
I could have stayed home that afternoon,
fallen ill, met your cousin instead of you

Someone else would have taken me that night
Isn't it better to be made of stone?
Or am I glad it was you?

It's better to be grass
People mow it, weed it and
it grows wild again, never the same.

4   Him

People say that a man
who has been bitten by a mad dog
sees the image of the beast
in water everywhere

Have the teeth of rabid love sunk into me,
that in the vastness of the sea, the river's
whirlpools and the glass from which I drink,
I cannot escape your image
smiling up at me?

5 Her

Marsha said, He's too old for you. Imagine!
Knock it off, I said. Next thing you'll say
I can't forget my dad. Come on!
But I still think Marsha's great. Lovely, really
'Cept when she gets like that...

You're old, my beetle, yes, but you find your way in me.
No one finds their way as easily as you.
Wait, I have to do my nails. Now? Yes, right this moment.
Wait, I said.

("I've got him where I want him,
like a beetle on a pin.")

9 Her

Dear bumpkin, I won't be beautiful when I'm old
Hurry,
caress the eyes of my breasts

22　Him

Yes, your eyes sparkle star-like everywhere!
And you make me your captive
when you dance with another!
It's true, it's true, your secret hair
burns on the lips of your lovers!

But soon (so very soon, my bunny rabbit)
you'll see them land on the moon on TV.
And what will still be shining then,
there in your room?
The diamond in your ear and nothing else.

from **The Sign of the Hamster** [1963]

Een razernij, een kuil, een pijnbank om te pijnen
Haar zotter lievers die nog in haar kercker zijn.
Bredero

(A pit, a frenzy, a rack on which to torture
the foolish lovers imprisoned in its dungeons.)

This is what I will write:
a trip from Ghent to Bruges and back.
Because I am being written.

It doesn't rain, it drizzles
in this country in the grip of the past.
Should I emigrate?

No rock or wilderness anywhere unless this history-crazed nation
excavates it and cultivates officers there to keep the peace
and nowhere is the thought's main seam laid bare.

This is what I was going to write:
a tater for later, a third for a verse,
allegro con fuoco.

    But peevishly grieving, the hooked spire rises,
    surrounded by clawing clouds and trees like antlers,
    under the aluminium sky with, in it, a falcon
    or a sparrow hawk.
    Tower, gallows, cross.

Now that—from the days of Ursula, her virgins and her executioner—
the plague has been reintroduced
to the cocked and loaded continent
I will be intelligibly resistible.

    Left Ghent
    —though I, thank God, do hate this town,
    there's not a turd that doesn't have a fly to buzz around it in the sun
    and Ghent has gates that never close
    although the Lys reeks of folklore (foreign currency)—
    for the town where I was born among cars,

scalpels and Memlincs.
Left not unwillingly,
but with women-trouble i.e. moody
and otherwise not contemplating heavenly bodies
but more the skin you pull over your own eyes
and the disease in which you find a home—satisfied.

Now the rabbits have died in the west
the foxes (giant hamsters) feed on the sheep,
biting their udders and bellies at night.

The sun wants its shadow.

Nocturnal birds of prey (so much softer than falcons or sparrow hawks)
wear lined gloves that cover
their fingers to the beds of their nails.

Like the cross spider's
simple rhymes.

Left Ghent among loaded smiling postmen,
following the tram tracks
"between channels, many"
and waving to relatives or residents.
Lots of streets offered diversions under skirts.
Low entertainment throbbed in wandering eyes.

Slow down, you, who used to
venerate the moment
and now return to *perhaps, therefore* and *but*
and will soon believe in Nature like a newspaper.

Cat people sleep away their days and hunt at night,
the birdman wakes before dawn,
I am the toad and nowhere to be found
unless you drag the pond
or beat the grass.
> The houses here are grey and crenelated,
> their skin recalls a woman with
> the pox. Renovation only speeds
> the rot. The houses here are dead and
> tortured The residents shack up in them
> quite happily.

Like using a scalpel
to search a vagina
for a foetus.

> Stefan George in Heidelberg: *You can ask me*
> *to eat bread that has been adulterated*
> *with a large amount of bark.*
> *That's acceptable.*
> *But there are situations in which one must say,*
> *"No, not that. I would rather die."*

> (Which? He doesn't hesitate,
> a mountain wind blows,
> the poet shines on a boy like the sun.)
> *"For instance.*
> *If one were obliged to eat rats or mice ."*

At that time (in the Bagne of Toulon)
they dyed the Zouaves' trousers
crimson.

Near South Station, in the Telstar, the card-players sit,
silhouetted sharply against the day.
Present are: Horsedick and Hadji Baba (because of his slanty eyes)
Gaspipe (for bashing passers-by) Snowwhite (four years suspended
sentence) and Bugs (who scratches)
cadaverous, sordid,
the weavers' shady descendants, joking
and hoping for a guardian angel to bring
them stunning luck and Sundays
(when they give the cards a rest)
udders.

In the Advanced Book Shop,
as academic as the lost Hebrew word in
Isaiah Two Six, as dark as Yahweh,
the toads are mating.
Her underneath, dropsical, with eyes of mud and chlorine,
and on her shoulders,
struggling yet motionless,
the father (like a suckling).
Blocked yet balanced.
No peat smoke can bother them. Gender is absent,
inflection and conjugation.
Then like a moral lesson, a celebration,
he moves, almost falls, gives a bitter belch and shudders. A tic.
Respect makes women thin. He moves no more.

Like the lure of your hedgehog
among plaster prickles.

Left for Bruges. The year has taken off its coat.
Rode through the countryside under azure skies, paling.
As always, the bandy-legged farmers came

to stare at the rain-bringing train,
bowing chastened to the ground.
No more than a legend, they dig the earth
like harnessed ploughshares. And vote compliantly.
Cherishing their farms and children Senator and priest
so sacred groaning wins over legislators
and no-one ever hits his neighbour, in astonishment
and fury at the sameness of things.
No-one vomits, skin rules and smothers the broad suspicions.
I don't want to go on, they are contagious, I want
to go back to being wrapped in the jabbering that dims as
Death defeats me.

Come here. Now? Come on. "Look into my eyes."

Bruges. My mother holds her babe—her prey—tight.
They have to search inside her.
The doctors at her bed compare makes of cars
and my father beeps at the gate.
Boneblack and dead I am born between
the hospital Memlincs,
Ursula among the angels wrapped in membranes.
No vine leaves or deerskin,
but metal organ pipes.
The seraphic canon: my first breastplate.

Again the year takes off its coat
in the city of lacework, obsequies and star-shaped vaults.
Oh, the old-style zinc smirks
of paladins, prelates and pimps

crammed onto panels!
On brick walls: the Annunciation.

Naked with a dagger and a feather hat: Lucrezia.
How elegantly mocking
is the past.
The fools of Bruges stand at the back
of the preaching hurtful mob.

Like the moth-
eaten myth.

[...]

from **Lord Wildboar** [1970]

Lord Wildboar

THE DEATH OF HIS FOREFATHER

He left us well before he died,
six months before, dull, broke, reeking, wrecked,
for all he walked intact from room to room.

"I haven't known a moment's joy,"
he said and tried to breathe,
audibly in the cooking smells.

He then turned blue. Like a plum.
He loved his plums. And cherries too,
the younger the better. Mother sat alone.

Not that he was dead just yet. No,
he held onto the chairs, seasick.
It was his heart that wouldn't die,

the engine. The chassis, the bodywork
were shot but the engine was still good.
He took to bed and sometimes he was dead.

The nuns hissed, "Yes, his time has come."
But with a gasp and a hiccup,
he started up again; just bluer.

They took him to the room
reserved for dying—
where the soul escapes decay.

His head was clearly shrinking,
the size now of a woman's fist.
With staring eyes. But could they see?

Nature takes its course. They stopped
his food and drink, but still he wanted it;
he chewed. The nuns sang the *Angelus*.

When they dabbed his lips with a sponge,
he bit into it and wouldn't let go.
They pinched his nose and he let go.

No rattle. A gasp and hiccup now and then.
Yes, his time had come. Freezing cold below the knees
and sweating up above. But the engine didn't stop.

They gave up bed baths. Turning him
might jolt his heart and make it stop.
Eau de Cologne, not too strong, on his temples.

Don't talk too loud. Don't mention debt.
Or signatures. Could you please leave now, sir.
Son or not, please leave. He hears it all, every word.

The inside of his mouth turned black. His skin—
the less said the better. They wiped away the black
that crept into the edges of the sores, so fast.

Fist-sized craters in the cheeks of his arse,
with black mouldy edges. Declutch, a shock, he over-
strained the engine. Which stopped, thank God.

And suddenly collapsed in on itself.
They filled the man-sized hole inside
with cardboard and cotton wool.

And wrenched him straight, before he stiffened,
or else they'd have to break the bones
to make him look good in the coffin.

No washing even now. Each touch disturbs
the flesh, as light as pollen in spring,
bone dust in the wounds.

Difficult sorrow came for Sir Wildboar,
beset by attorneys and family meetings
and the days of the cart and the funeral.

I was the nail in his coffin, he often said.
Even now, a fingernail, as a final gesture,
scratching the walnut of his head.

Lord, take your son into your arms.
The women went left (all lovers).
The men went right (all sons).

The time of the earth fermenting inside him now.
The time of the seasons. Quick give me a beer.
Forefathers galore—and all cut off.

His Prayers

The slow cattle of my days
and all those years of rancour,
bad-tempered romps in the garden next door.

I dreamt I unzipped my lashes
and gave them to you, merciful one,
and you blew them like a dandelion,
oh, restrain your punishing hand!

In my subterranean warehouse of words
the iron jams, the plum bursts open,
teeth chip and splinter.
Your holy bread won't heal me.

Nails, thorns and Veronica's veil.
And how the guts of the three murderers
on Golgotha dried out, the third one's too!
Your will be done!

The temple curtain works itself loose,
falling over my eyes, my lips, my crotch
through the intercession of all your mutilated children.

2

It's later than anyone imagines.
What's growing in our core?
What's gnawing on our backbone?
We carry our skin.

 —Benevolent one.

And we are not scorched
though darkness falls
in the stairwell of thought
and night splits the tips of our fingers.

 —Look down in mercy.

Warts from earlier crimes
are planted in the child
in its mother's womb.
Quick. Slide Father under the bed,
put on a crash helmet.

 —I place myself
 at your disposal.

3

The house rustles, a board snaps loose like a shot.
Then someone says my name,
nearby, more clearly than my mother used to call
in the darkening street.

Clattering leaves,
animals lapping water,
and my name again,
like the bark of a birch bursting open.

Listening to the muffled tick
accelerating in my wrist
I wait for the order that will now
descend from a hellish flock of crows.

Demolish the house, brick by brick?
Quell the embryo inside of her?
What must I incinerate?
How to smother forever the prayer
rattling around my bed?

from **Hearsay** [1970]

Anthropology

This nation that supposedly
moves between two poles,
excess and godliness,

believes less in the hereafter
than in its daily groats.

This nation will give alms on Sunday
for the pope or Africa,

or burn incense to venerate the statue
of the Curé d'Ars who stank of the poor,

but generally pays and prays to calm
its fear of leaner years and butter up
its docile rulers, the realtors.

In Flanders Fields

The soil here's the richest.
Even after all these years without manure
you could grow a dead-man's leek
to beat the best.

The British veterans grow scarce.
Each year they point out to their scarcer friends:
Hill Sixty, Hill Sixty-One, Poelcapelle.

In Flanders Fields the threshers drive
in ever tighter rings around the winding lines
of hardened sandbags, the bowels of death.

The local butter
tastes of poppies.

Memorial Statue in West Flanders

The grazing of the nearby cattle.
The farmer sitting in the shade of the pale statue.
The trees that bow for the wind from the sea.

His parents bought the patch of land
where he was buried in mud up to the jawbone.
He was a gifted student.
"Maths or something," the farmer says.

The sculptor worked from an old school photo.
"Two years later the parents died as well," the farmer says.
"It's getting cold. I have to milk the goats."

More bones somewhere else.
Corroded by the acid of the polder soil,
a childless son with a guilty stare,
as if looking down at his geometry,
his grave in the grass.

A Bed In Bruges

"I work in the chemical industry, Sir,
where you die by degrees.
After ten years you get to retire
because of the fumes in your lungs.

"I've been there fourteen years, Sir,
the last two as a driver.
And in those two years I haven't had to vomit once,
because of the fresh air.

"We Belgians drive better than anyone else in all of Europe,
and I've been everywhere.
Because we drive dangerously.
It makes you more careful of the others,
who drive dangerously too, but won't admit it.

"And you know the most beautiful thing I've seen?
And I've been in the Sistine Chapel,
and I've seen Gisele lift her skirts in the Mocambo.
Well, it's in a shop in Bruges,
a wine-red bed. Empire. Or is it Louis Quinze?

"In that bed, with Gisele, I would forget my three children
and the entire calendar.
Love, Sir, should be in satin.
And death, Sir, is the feeling you get in your stomach
when you know you will never be able to afford a bed like that."

The Farmers

Thirty pigs, fifteen cows, a tractor 75 HP,
a TV, fifty chickens, no kids.
    ("We'd have liked some, sure, Sir,
    but we're not keen on doctors or hospitals,
    'cause what if something happened to the wife, Sir,
    who'd take care of the stock?")

Villas—"Morning Glory", "Spring Breeze", "Bambino"—
are planted in their fields.
Their rye and wheat dissected by
the Flemish Touring Club's recommended walking path.

Sundays, after Mass, they shuffle,
wearing shirts, transformed, clean-shaven, awkward, over their fields,
staring at the earth they don't see on workdays,
with their short-sighted grubbing and grabbing.

Potatoes and bacon weekdays
and every Sunday a chicken out of the freezer.
When the air boils and the crows are gasping, they drink seven
slugs of brown ale
leaning on the oil tank in front of the house.

They only tremble after a day tossing hay up over their heads,
or filling in the deposit slip at the Municipal Credit.
("Three to three and a half percent. Is it safe?
The notary says it is. But what if they get in trouble, Sir?")

Does the tolling of the village bell
preserve them from their fate? To avert the evil eye they nail three
bats to the barn door, alive.

The Rubens Room
in the Antwerp Museum of Fine Arts

Faced with so much irrepressible flesh, the girl in the museum smiles
like a young nun in the sun.
Such excessiveness is hardly human;
the human, as her ethics teacher taught her,
is a mammal, true, but these women,
this endless flood of fleshy quince (the perfect bridal fruit)? No,
the girl laughs. She hugs her *Avenue* to her breasts,
two underdone fried eggs with lots of runny white.

Does she have the same tissues?
Will a similar surrender one day melt her skeleton
into such filthy, sloppy tumescence?

If this blubber is divine,
then life's a thing that suffocates in gravy and jelly
with udders and tangled hair,
a thing that strangles by embrace.

The girl laughs. Chastity, as far as she's concerned, can triumph over love
and death can triumph over chastity.
The vulva deificata is a different commodity,
installed in her it's quite a different thing,
a whisper, rather, in the night in spring.

1965

(in reply to a newspaper survey about the previous year)

Year of atrocities, year of TV screens and stock reports,
Year of milk and honey if you're asleep,
Year that weighs on your stomach if you're awake,
Sweet year, good year for sleep-walkers,
Year that 25 billion Belgian francs went to NATO
for tanks, flags and jets
        (mosquitoes in death's unbounded clouds)
Year of Mobutu, we send him assistance in dollars and cents knowing
they'll
        blossom into percentages,
Year of Voeren, which people want to rescue for a language they only read
in
        advertisements,
Year of freeways for ever hastier sheep,
Year of rot in Belgian skulls,
Year that licked at the trough of folklore,
Year (fortunately far from our piggy banks and our folk dancing)
        of the escalation there where children grey with fear
        dig themselves deeper into mud
        (Give them this day our daily napalm
        and later our canned food and later our prayers)
Year that freezes smiles.

That was the year I went to live in a village
with books, a woman and a child
that grows
while I tell stories about tigers in the East.

Home

III

The singular sky
That brightens the earth.

The path that leads our steps
And in it our track: a dotted line to the end.

Nature: bordered.
The land: bound in.
In shades of salmon and metal.

The posts that sway when you move.
The reflection of the saffron field.

The pigeon behind wire.
The mouse-grey on the floor of the cage
Is the old seeds.

Speckled and striped.
The world seems trapped in a grid.
Your eyes pierce the pattern,
Mottled, almost hidden,
The hole is a mirror.

The simplicity of a bucket.

And finally, awake, present,
Never ready-varnished, only limited

By walls of gradual lines,
Turning on the spot,
The man bending down to his bucket.

Home. Almost a world of its own.

In Memory of Ferdi

In the Paris I now hate,
in '55, in rooms that were scorching,
we were hungry,
you showed a lot of breast that summer—
Your lips: scornful of all others.

You're in the night now and in water
and I—do you believe me? am senseless, sleepless.
You who made velvet ferns
in what I must call "back then".

Even now you confuse my thoughts of you.
They flake and chip, chattering away
in this disenchanted canto for a slight, lost lady

Ah, the emptiness of my regret
and the wandering desperation
of my provisional present tense
with you in many coats, flowering flesh
in the bygone, bygone zone.

Female Friend

She said, "I would never kill.
　　Not even if a man a meter away from me
　　was strangling my little boy.
　　All life is sacred."

And I saw her in sodium light,
the sibyl with her outrageous law,
in heat with suicide and prayer.

How the clay hungers for the skeleton
and the earth for the dung
and the mop for the blood!
And how I dance in my bestial sweat
and would kill and how!

Early December

(for the New Year's guests)

Shall I ask them for New Year's? To celebrate together here
With punch and feeble grins? To see the New Year in.
Who? Not those who are too wild, not those who are too mild,
Not those who count too much, but those who tell too much.

And most of all the ones like us.
I will soothe them with booze until they crack.
Should I make them pay? Would that enhance their thirst?
Quail? Waffles? Shall I also ask the self-generating

Toad full of poison gas who guesses at family secrets
In my transparent verse? And the greasy connoisseur
Who sits up and begs at the slightest crumb of protestation?
And that shrunken beetle who writes in his paper so brashly

To deny the migration of souls in my poetry? Ah,
Even his corpse will never crack a smile!
I will invite them. No, you ask them, *madame*, as
I, homunculus in my menthol cloud of dread,

Am like Mickey Spillane, weathered out of my own desires.
Ah, together we will all compulsively pig ourselves
To a full-blown rectal cancer,
We, miniatures more at home in heraldry

Than in nature. Ah, to greet the New Year with
All its whims and grudges, its freezing cold, we'll scream
dozens of Quantanamèras and Yesterdays.
Yes, *again, again.* Shall I ask them?

Diary Pages

6   (*On Thomas's Fourth Birthday*)

Later, my son, you'll be a man,
later you will yearn to learn the how and why.
They'll stamp you like luggage.
They'll hurt you for your wishes and your dreams.
And you will try once and for all to photograph
the how and why of the woman
        who turns between your sheets
        who sings as you expand in her skin.
And later still, son, your life
will be a scrapbook.
But not for ages yet, no, not for ages yet.

17 (*Translation*)

Translated Borges's *Tango* today.
(*qua propter quod bene factum est in una lingua*)
Jesus!
It creaks in every joint, it waddles,
this dirge of a dance.
In Spanish: a hard box with music inside,
       a sparking flint, a coiled spring.
In Flemish: a band-aid. The metre slides under the table.
       The link to the music is lost.
(*non est possibile*)
Faithfully ailing, how else could it be?
A Flemish tango on two-timing feet.

from **Morning, You** [1971]

*Mad Dog Stanzas, traditionally reserved for
poetry by drunkards and lunatics*

I see her thinking: My kisses
are cold tonight.—How she then hurls
herself into that trusted void!
Mechanically prodding me from
her vacuum.—Towards her smell.

I count the steps on the stairs
and then subtract her age.
The number of times the clocks strike
are the thirteen letters of her name.
I tear her like a wet newspaper.

Will I ever grow used to time
that wears us down together?
Or will I, like her, become a coincidence,
an aperture in time?—
Her slit is my sign.

You lie there naked, but no more naked than at the doctor's.
Your wound no more naked than your knees.
As if it's a habit. My own body, I've come to see
with different eyes. As if, after all these years,
the rejection no longer applies.

Your palm glides more softly, you're starting
to get it. Your breasts are fuller too
after three months of caresses. The dance
of your hip finally echoes our first nights
with all those teething problems.

Close to her, I think: our story is
cold metal, something for half
a day a week, a passing madness.
And I'm just the table leg a bitch
pisses on out of longing for something else.

Getting dressed. Pressing what I've worshipped
into stretch panties. Arranging your segments.
You raise your foot & I think
you think I'm a part of you.
Something like an ingrown toenail.

"More. Don't stop. Faster!" No, she didn't groan
it, she swore, "Oh, God, oh, God damn it!"
And then, "What have you done
to my face? It looks years younger!"
And then, "Oh, boy, if you ever cheat on me!"

It's finished. Adieu. Hidden under make-up.
Or rather, did it ever exist? Or is there
a corpse still lying here between the sheets,
looking like the two of us and panting still?
Her mouth: my lock.

The smell of her cunt and arse confuse her,
the taste in my mouth shames her.
She's not that fish, she thinks, with piss and sweat,
but some other animal, deodorised and in another land.
That's why she's sometimes hated by her glands.

Her name which you say and yawning
spell out over and over again, snowed under.
Her name which you groan
until the neighbour calls the police.
Her name which you swallow / like she swallows her pill.

When she sleeps I open
her finest pages and read
the wiring of her soft,
warm television—
a circuit from her to her.

Ha-ha! I had a heart, I swear it,
trembling like any other. And chattering.
Truly, it lay there waiting for her.
—She took her iron and placed
it on my heart and pressed and pressed.

"Do you want to?"—*"If you do, so do I."*
"Then I don't want to."—*"Me neither."*
Who wanted to? Who wanted to?
When tenderness is in the majority,
there's no one to open the door.

"He took my virginity," she said.
"Every day I'm scared of him," she said.
"I can never trust him," she said.
"I sob for hours at a time," she said and sobbed,
"and you, you're just my lover."

from **Figurative** [1973]

Five Polaroids of Jesus Christ

I

A stick insect
with something feminine around the ribs
an iris in his midriff.

> *(Death is in my hipbone, the left,*
> *my jaws already calcified;*
> *once I was as bright as a flower,*
> *as bitter as blossom.)*

Mutant. Transformed from man
to mantis by paternal wrath.
He is edible, digestible
like the crickets of the sea.

The sun burns him
to blisters and shreds
and ash that drifts to the water.

2

At the village pump he let the children
play with his crown of thorns.

He pointed at a comet and said,
"Look, my father's winking at you."

Then his mount grew restless.
"I would like," he said, *"the greatest sinner
among you to take a bite out of my ear."*

But they kept staring at his girlish hair
and sullenly he spurred his pony on
across the crushed-ice sand.

3

One of his manifestations preached
the following: "Hey, followers!
What's going on? People,
God help us, with the hots for purity,
want to replace gold with white!
They want to shuck off their senses,
unsullied by minerals, changing
the gold of thought
into bland half-hearted white!
As if my father's hair
was not curled and gilded!
As if indulgences and repentance
earn you immortality!
Forget it.
God is in gold alone
and gold is the only reason
for an almost reasonable smile."

4

"Burdened with crown and armour,
wrapped in my tentacles,
braggart and beggar,
I preached mercy and yearning.
I could bear no emptiness.

"Now I no longer turn my cheek.
I stink like a bed full of lovers
and stiff as a ram
I sometimes dance with fury.

"I only pray when I shit
(and no longer as the Son of Someone).
(What's more, the Slut is dead.)
I only pray that it will end."

5

When he felt the first cold
in his pores and glands
he told parables to his contemporaries
and sang psalms for the poor.

Sometimes he stopped breathing
and said to his father, "*I thirst.*"
When the evenings grew shorter each year
he practised dying.

He only ever coupled
with his mother's hat.

Ulysses

I have seen too many battles,
heard too many lovers' howls,
I always travelled too far.

A diorama has replaced my eye,
a humming top my ear.

Too much mud,
too many corpses in it.
Too much joy.

I will now hide among the suitors,
those beggars.

A Kind of Goodbye

I

A snail trail. That's all there is to say
that I came by, a Wednesday.
You don't need to forget yourself,
others forget for you.

And yet: as dark as it was in my ferns,
        as white as I once saw the sea,
        as cowardly as I died and as often,
there can't have been a single person.
Didn't you see me?

Who's coughing? It's my throat, that's all.
Really, no.—I never saw you.

5

They say you've blinded me.
Probably.

Although it's mostly misty when I lunge
at the sound of your hissing

and often the wind from your mouth is cooling
as I kiss.

You said, "Let me be your whore,"
and I asked, "What does that make me?"

You said, "I'll give you three guesses."

I guessed: a moment,
a wish, a possibility.

And knew: a pilot light,
an attic full of rags,
yes, a festive hockshop.

And for the others, and there weren't many,
a ground beetle
rummaging briefly in their hair,
an itch, hardly a breath.

Introbo

I should go in to you? To you, you sleepwalker?
To ask your forgiveness? Forget it.

Must I erase my sleeping sickness
with midnight masses?

I want no peace with you,
and no prayers to you,

I recognise no dear lord,
I'm not a servant anymore,

Even if I
could see you,
I would decline
your thorns, your thirst, your death, your stench.

Hecate Speaks

Only the incomplete
makes me replete and fat.
Beauty is not harmony.

Most of it, I must forswear,
and all of it, allay.
My shadow is the only thing
that doesn't make me shy.

Even if you take my arm,
even if you're very warm,
even if I have no choice
beyond your fingers, nose and cheek,
even if my belly swells for you
even if you bring me in from the cold,
even if you shut your mouth,
even if I grow in your earth,
I still won't let myself be caught,
between your gallows and garrotte.

Stay in your wood,
where people thrive.
I don't want to walk there,
hawk there, be pushed underwater there.
I won't surrender my shell,
my shadow, my husk.

XI

I hear with my little ear
something that I don't hear.
Whoever wants to hear me
must speak with my mouth.
Who's this? Me.
And you?

I see that you think
that I just screamed,
and you heard no sound.

I see that you hope
that I called
for help perhaps.

It was my throat,
it wasn't me,
it was my playful voice box,
my sweetheart,

or my rutting grief.
But it, Father, was not me.
Not once in all the days of your life
will you know that kind of delight.

XIII

Saying I hoped to eventually make bird!
Crippled wings and all!

Saying I wanted to save myself
through mortification and lies!

I wanted indemnity,
I wanted distraction,
in my secure sick bay
full of shells from the old days
yesterday's dressings
and tomorrow's toe nails,

waiting for someone to come
and sew me back together
with gossamer, angel hair.

I've been spoilt in my tent of pain.
I believe I'm smiling.

from Almanac [1982]

ALMANAC
LIAR'S SACK

Tout homme digne de ce nom
A dans le coeur un serpent jaune
Baudelaire *(l'Avertisseur)*

I

Begin this year in glory
and hear what the young father,
hoarse and red,
whispers to his first-born:
                         "Leave and dread."

5

It's fine for Dad to hit me
because Dad likes to
with his hand of hard wood.
If I was big and fat,
I'd do it too, if I could,
to a kid
who loves his dad as much as I do.

12

"If you get married, you'll hit rock bottom,"
my mother said,
and I felt it at once, that layer of rock,
under the soles of my seven-league boots.

20

He slammed the door.
Never going back.
Not if she put him on a throne.
But by the time he crossed the tracks
he was tired and his feet were sore.
He thought, "No-one's made of stone."

22

—Just go away.
To your mother or something.
—There is no or something.
—To your mother then.
—She's dead.
—Oh, poor thing. A long time now?
—Since before I was born.

24

A she-ape, but bald,
that's what I call her.
It's not exactly flattering,
but what can I do,
it happens to be true,
especially at three in the morning.

31

"You alone can help me," she said.
"Help me. Make me forget him."

That night, when she moaned,
I thought of him in that far land
and she heard it and turned to stone.

74

They carried off the victim.
They took the pimp into custody.
Then the mounted policeman
gave the whore
some more of the third degree.

100

"How can I ever get warm,"
she cried,
"with this ice-cold snake inside of me?"

The old man sat on the cow
without a stitch of clothing on.
He'd had it to here with the world by now
but the cow went on and on.

from **Shards**

Montale's "Little Testament"

For Harry

That which at night like a will-o'-the-wisp
lightens the skullcap of my thought,
the mother-of-pearl trail of the snail
or the glittering dust of crushed glass
is no church light, no office light
that's fed
by a clerk, either black or red.

All I can leave behind for you
is this rainbow, this iris,
the only witness to a faith
that has been battered,
a scraping of hope that burnt slower
on the hearth than green hardwood.

And so, Harry, keep this spectrum,
this iridescent pollen,
in your pocket mirror
when all the lamps have been extinguished,
when hell has broken loose,
when a dark lucifer lands, exhausted,
on a bend in the Thames, the Hudson, the Seine,
shakes the pitch from his wings
and says, This is the hour.

It is no inheritance, no talisman
that can keep the cobwebs of memory intact
through the wet, hot wind of summer.
(A story can only survive in ash.
Perseverance is tantamount to annihilation.)

Righteous was your sign.
Those who have seen it can only
find you. Each recognises his own.

Your haughtiness was no flight,
your humility was not low
when you lit your *black light* somewhere far away
there was no smell of sulphur.

from Alibi [1985]

Halloween

I

It is as quiet as the death of the dead no one knows
everywhere outside of your room,
where you dance all alone like before.
But there too I hear
what you don't say
the way I want to hear it.
Far from bedraggled Europe,
where the deathly haze will soon descend,
we stare at each other,
almost dead like plastic chairs,
and neither you nor I admits the murder of me or you.

II

Lying on the black rubber floor,
the autumn leaf, yellowed over the weekend.
Greedily you nibble on an ice cube
shaped like a heart.
November comes and brings the bitter half
of the year in with it.
Time to reconsider.
If I were a bog body, would you love me?
Senile, would you laugh at me?
You nibble on me, but not really,
I'm too old and cold for that.
Cupid, a little brat made of cement,
arrives on cue and smashes to pieces on the floor.

III

Mountains with coyotes and rattlesnakes,
in the valley, the stinking cars,
and in the bed with twelve pillows, you on your back.
You too will lose your shine and your teeth,
but not this afternoon.
Although your mumbling has already paled
as you stumble short-sightedly out of bed.
You, once made of marble, with hair sprayed green,
grow more and more absorbed
in a story about yourself
even while listening like a blind woman
for, somewhere overseas, the *beep*
of the alarm in the watch on your lover's wrist.

V

What I know on the eve of November first?
That hemp should be sown at midnight,
that last week you tasted of ginger,
that the great cold will descend on a night like tonight,
that you smile at me like a cross-eyed nurse,
that the sun seeds cancer in the lung, the moon in the womb,
that it's time to burn all the cardboard boxes
from the old days before I forget,
that everyone feeds off someone else,
that you're like the hills of Carmel,
shining and salty as the sea,
my hobbled doe, my model with a dose,
my nun who hungers for clothes and mirrors and
the orgasms of men who growl,
and that you groan in your sleep without me.

Even Now

*The four-lined stanzas are based
on a selection from the Sanskrit
poem the* Chaurapanchasika.
*Some of the commentary is
Paul Valéry's.*

I

Even now, gagged and bound on the gallows today,
she, who will awaken soon with swollen lips, eyes closed,
was something I knew, and then lost sight of, and how,
but how did I lose her, how does a dog bark when it's drunk ?

Sanskrit horniness in syllabic lines?
Bring it on,
for me, it's as clear as a monad:
all seduction comes from seeing,
from the action of seeing or from the idea,
or rather the sensation that we've missed something.

II

Even now, her face like the moon and her body like the moon,
young, bitter young, with those breasts and buttocks and ribs.
Love had arrows once, a quiver full, you felt how sharp they were,
a torment, you were sure, for that full white moon of hers.

To put it another way,
seduction creates a necessity
that had not existed previously
or was drowsing, asleep.

III

Even now, her chewed-down nails, her chafed nipples,
the creamy thighs and, in between, her vertical smile,
and she who despised metaphysics said, "Ah, honey,
every cell of your come contains both God and his mum."

"So she exists in a world
of autumn crocuses."
"No, she is an autumn crocus, really and completely."
"Sir, science requires categories."
"Her red pussy, the arch of her back,
are they categories?"
"Um, yes, but almost abstract,
like an autumn crocus by Van Doesburg."

IV

Even now, the welts and bruises, swellings and tattoos,
love's injuries hidden underneath her flimsy frock,
and I fear this will just go on and on, this bitter furtive
scratching and clawing at her miniature no-man's-land.

We're forgetting two things, by God,
the different ways of being
and the different ways of not being.
I fear that you're trapped between no longer being
and not yet having been. What do you say to that?

V

Even now, completely still, she lay excessively alone,
abandoned left and right, a numbness in the roof of her mouth,
and I, as motionless as her in my own cell, heard
the clink and rattle of the chain around her ankle.

"When will you be together?" my mother asked.
I said, "In the realm of King Baudouin,
when the world will be truthful,
when the Yellow River is clear,
in a month of Sundays,
at the noon of midnight?"

VI

Even now, I remember how, in the morning, tired and slow
after making languid love, she hung her head almost shyly,
a duck that slid over the lake and nipped at the water,
before diving down and biting me and then never again.

You could also say, "The roots seek what's clammy,
the blades find the sun
and the plant forms itself
between two equilibriums,
between one longing and the other."

VII

Even now, I tie her pitch-black hair up in cocky
combs, plumes and quills and worship her as a totem
and a cross in my house that quickly, awkwardly
transforms into a temple to Love, the furtive goddess.

Soldiers painted a cross
on their shields and won the battle.
But you're in thrall to a game
where only losing counts.

VIII

Even now, all those rooms and nights and creamy nakedness
and all that sleeping after and before and the smell of heather.
How she snored when I asked if she was happy now and how
she stroked the bolster that had ended up between us.

Until the eighth century
one kissed the Pope's hand.
But then there was a woman who kissed his hand
and wouldn't let go.
That very night the Pope chopped that hand off.
That's why one now kisses his feet.

IX

Even now, her limbs, all four of them at work, exhausted,
and her freshly-washed hair hanging down over her warm cheeks
as she grabbed my neck with her ankles, a giggling executioner,
beheaded, presenting me with the cool and glistening wound.

Just as the cell shapes itself to its minuscule prey,
obeying that which it will consume
and warming itself on its pseudopods,
uniting with it.
Admit it, admiration is called for.

X

Even now, I raise a flag and put my arms up in the air,
crying, "Comrade!" But she was the one who surrendered.
Because on the battlefield I heard her splutter and rage
in her mother's accent, uttering filthy syllables.

Love, cinders and scrap metal,
bread and water
love, wake up
and approach from the void
that freezes me.

XI

Even now, when I am on the verge of crossing over
to that other life, she leads me as through black water,
ogling me and leering at me through her dangerous lashes,
laughing at me as I, drenched through, ascend her golden bank.

Above all else, without exception,
the forest path we follow is a labyrinth.

XII

Even now, her body is carmine and gleaming with sweat,
her openings all smooth and slippery with baby oil.
Yet what I know of her remains a strange gesture,
a thing with no echo, full of bitterness, chance and remorse.

Professor Policard said, "It's so hot!
I have the impression a certain heaviness
has entered our synapses,
that in weather like this our neurons swell."

XIII

Even now, I forget about the gods and their ministers,
she is the one who shatters, condemns and forgets me,
she, who is of all seasons but especially the winter,
growing colder and more beautiful the more I die.

Why don't you say anything about the coldness of silence?
The self-satisfied destructive silence of Ajax,
Iole, Niobe, Achilles, you name it,
all prayers I wrote in my dotage
despite knowing better.

XIV

Even now, among all women there is not one like her,
not one whose furious mouth surprised me so much.
My foolish soul would tell of her if it were able,
but my soul has been plundered and razed to the ground.

And with the self-assurance of sleepwalkers
we keep skirting the issue.

XV

Even now, how she quivered with exhaustion and whispered,
"Why are you doing this? I will never let you go, my king."
There was no colder monarch than me and recklessly
I showed her how the King's one eye was watering.

*Antony van Leeuwenhoek to the President of the Royal
Society in November 1677:
"What I investigate is only what,
without sinfully defiling myself,
remains as a residue after conjugal coitus."*

XVI

Even now, when I dare to think of my lost bride,
my legs tremble beneath me imagining who plucks her now,
my wandering oleander of a bride who won't stop tearing
the weed that I am out of her garden of delight.

If you dare to think? Although while
constructing a consistent image
of your lady,
you forget time, mass and velocity!
Strange. Eros: a blind photographer.

XVII

Even now, with the bees of death swarming around me
I taste the honey of her belly and hear the buzz
of her orgasm and stare at the moist rose
petals of her pulsing carnivorous flower.

These symbols are multiplying
at an alarming rate. They're a threat to existence itself.
Can't the babbling in our tower of Babel
be a little clearer?
Maybe you should limit your writing,
do it on the wall.

XVIII

Even now, our wide bed that reeks of her and her armpits,
our pale bed shat upon by the birds of the world.
At the bird market she said, "I want that one, the wild one,
the one that can't stop tapping its beak on that tit of hers."

  It is dangerous to believe
  that you understand the least bit of it.
  Much more than the unknown,
  you should fear the known.

XIX

Even now, the way she resisted and refused my mouth,
lying limply only after I had floored her with my nails
in her breast, and then, while I slept, drunk on her abundance,
stoking me up again like a fire that had long seemed dead.

You can see it like this:
the physical corset in which a beetle grows
is responsible for the mental straitjacket
that regulates its patterns of behaviour.

XX

Even now, her supple breasts lying in my hands
and her lips thick from my nipping, biting teeth
and her chewed-down nails and her chafed nipples,
and how she squinted in the cruel light of morning.

"Now, now," said Monsieur Paul
"Speculative thought never imagined
what the microscope has seen.
Come now, le vent se lève. Il faut tenter de vivre."

XXI

Even now, I tell myself that in the straitened time
between me and the Arctic night, she was the stars,
the grass, the cockroaches, the fruit and the maggots,
and how I accepted this and how it delights me yet.

The beauty
who gives you the greatest pleasure,
what is her purpose?
At most she'll scare the fish
when she jumps in the water.

XXII

Even now, how to describe her, what to compare her to?
Until I'm in my grave I will arrange her and paint her
and spoil her and, head spinning, blow her back to life
with my irritating complaints, my nerve-wracking moaning.

"You can say that again!
But I sympathise. After all natives
paint their faces
to protect themselves from the sun."

XXIII

Even now, with her mascaraed lashes and her eye shadow
and her painted lips and her scarlet earlobes pierced.
"I'm burning up," she said, "I can't go on, I'll murder you,
those fingers of yours, nobody else ever, nowhere, never."

Not seeing something for what it is
is more treacherous
than faulty reasoning.

XXIV

Even now, she's still nineteen despite how much she drinks,
and though the tracks of far too many tears have worn wrinkles
in her cheeks, carving through her camouflage and war paint,
the mould and freezing cold of her life without me.

We should examine
her biorhythm, her hormonal ebb and flood,
the behaviour of her enzymes, blood sugar and amino acids
when you're not around.

XXV

Even now, if I could find her again as a fairytale
from the moon after a cloudburst and lick her toes again,
back on the road with my heart of stone I fear it would lead
to another horribly soppy song à la Cole Porter.

I've seen many a heart,
being a coroner, and I've yet to see one
that's worn out nicely at the same rate
as the other organs.

XXVI

Even now, her more than the water in her miraculous body,
a salt lake on which a duck would float and stay
and that duck with a dick was me hear me quack!—and she
being a lake rocked me on her surging waves or pretended.

This is completely at odds with physics.
Although physics itself can also be seen as a protest
against the cult of common sense.

XXVII

Even now, if I could see her again with that short-sighted look
of hers, heavier around the hips and with a bigger bum,
I would, I believe, embrace her again and drink from her again,
a bee could not be happier, busier, lither and more limber.

Seduction changes us, obviously,
because we are
titillated, incited, spurred on
by one of our possibilities with that one possibility,
that spitfire,
determining the whole
and completely sweeping it, her, us, along.

XXVIII

Even now, with me entangled and knotted together with her,
the Destroyer is at work and scorching mankind.
People of standing are lost and cannot find their way
as after a battle without weapons or winners.

Even now, wearing her shackles and with the bloody nose
of a lover, I say, filled with her blossoming spring,
"Death, stop torturing the earth. Don't wait, dear death,
for me to come, but follow her lead and strike hard!"

Envoi

My poems stand around yawning.
I'll never get used to it. They've lived here
long enough.
Enough. I'm kicking them out, I don't want to wait
until their toes get cold.
I want to hear the throb of the sun
or my heart, that treacherous hardening sponge,
unhindered by their clamour and confusion.

My poems aren't a classic fuck,
they're vulgar babble or all too noble bluster.
In winter their lips crack,
in spring they go flat on their back on the first hot day,
they ruin my summer
and in autumn they smell of women.

Enough. For twelve more lines on this page,
I'll keep them under my wing
then give them a kick up the arse.
Go somewhere else to beat your drum and rhyme on the cheap,
somewhere else to tremble in fear of twelve readers
and a critic who's asleep.

Go now, poems, on your light feet,
you haven't stamped hard on the old earth,
where the graves grin at the sight of their guests,
one body piled on the other.
Go now and stagger off to her
who I don't know.

from **Sonnets** [1986]

If my slight Muse do please these curious days,
The pain be mine, but thine shall be the praise.

SHAKESPEARE, *Sonnet 38*

I

That almost everything attains perfection
for just a little moment and then snuffs out
accords with both the world and Einstein's theory.
And that people grow like plants

under a single polluted sky
and decay together equally in memory
is guaranteed by the selfsame time
that's breathing down my neck.

That's why I must now desperately
sing the praises of that one night
I saw you on display,

your youthful enchantment unparalleled,
a naked monument with full impunity,
toppling over before my sight.

III

I thought (I'm often such a swine):
I'll wait until the winter comes
and carves its lines around her mouth,
or for deceitful spring to envy her

and dig deep trenches in the field of her skin,
then she, like me, will bear the signs.
But suddenly this fall arrived, hazy, bright,
confusing and as blessed as my late love

and you remained unharmed, my love.
I even dared to entertain the thought
that the cold inside of me might never reach you,

and that you will never leave my side,
in horror at my deep-freeze breath. I believed it.
The way a bleeding corpse might still believe.

XIII

Sometimes I pray for a speedy death,
knowing that things of value must always beg,
that follies flourish all around
and truth falls here on barren ground.

The missiles of a scandalous encampment
are celebrated.
The laws of a treacherous government
are decorated.

Virtue is exhausted.
Evil is the captain.
Adieu, my swamp of a land

I want to sink like a stone.
So why don't I do it?
It is too soon to leave her here alone.

XIV

When the copper kettle with the ash
of what I was is shaken upside-down
above the patient grass, my love,
don't stand there like a clown.

Wipe the mascara from your face
and think of the fingers that wrote these lines
in the days we ached for each other,
and stroked you when they were still alive.

And laugh at what I was, and don't forget
the snoring in the cinema,
the underpants that kept on slipping down,

the stupid jokes and the lumbering gait
that always brought me back to you
to take you in your warm abundance.

from **The Traces** [1993]

The Traces

of the one who tripped over his bag
of the blind man and the treed cat
of her name in the snow

The traces
of a life that couldn't be a work of art
of preoccupied
and suddenly mottled hands
and a bruised pancreas that same week

The traces
of loss but no carping about that
even the ivy loses its suckers

The traces
of his father's coat that was once a tent
for him and his broken tomahawk

The traces
of Mozartkugeln, being such a sweet tooth,
even for Milchrahmensahmenstrudel

The traces
of the fire-brigade siren and 5 Megatons
over Antwerp and the vomiting rats
one hundred dead boy scouts in the cellar
around the corner

The traces
of golden children's tears: the resin of the cypress
of the tortoise shot to pieces

The traces
    of the one who praised fragmentation
    even though he clung to simplicity
    him with his basketful of answers

The traces
    of the dead bodies he climbed over
    the mossy statues he gripped tight
    the sheep with their false teeth

The traces
    in haste, in innocence too
    as incongruous as that sounds
    (he was a poet for a few years
    but don't ask when)

The traces
    of goodbye of course
    goodbye to Glenfiddich, toothache, sunglasses
    strangers sobbing in bed

The traces
    of the one who wasn't present enough here
    and remained unreconciled
    in compassion too

The traces
    of what was once a poem
    mostly a comparison
    and now a corpse of words
    to one day thaw

The traces
    of the one who specialised
    in the sheepishness of love
    because he saw that expectation in her eyes

The traces
    of his singing saw
    of a begging tomcat
    of the collapsing plastic skeleton
    of the sea finally without a murmur

Poet

Autumn. Listen. Clicking. Do you hear that deep clattering?
It's coming closer: in our clothes, in our hair.
We're lousy with sound. What is this leprous muttering?
Child, it's only the poets outside with their teeth chattering.

The closer the poets get to their dying,
The more furiously they groan at the stars.
In the morning mist that melts their metaphors,
The poets freeze in their recognizable sports coats.

Hear how feverishly they explain their approaching demise,
Struggling to render their rattling transparent,
To ensure that their widowed readers are moved to tears.

"Oh, our egos were way too obscure!" they moan.
"The times required it, as multi-interpretable as we ourselves!"
And look, they're crawling out of their souls' bandages,
Mouths full of wine and cheese and pleas for mercy,
For their prostatism, their plagiarism.

One foot in the grave, the poets suddenly discover
The calming miracles of gods, aphorisms and aspirins,
Of tenderness. For the first time his sweetheart
Can read with her lips something her sweetheart has written.

And before the poets, wasted winter apples
Scorned as too scrawny by the pickers,
Finally fall in November,
They want the neighbours to understand that fall
For posterity. In dairy words, ripening to mush like a pear.

Embittered, they keep listening for the crumpling
Of the newspaper that persists in misspelling their names,
Filling in their crossword puzzles
With anecdotes, anxiety and stumbling love.

But too late, too deaf, the poets realise
That what was dark and dull in their poems
Will not grow lighter through wear, with time,
But keeps on rotting. As unfathomable as ever:
Their homes, their words, the equator, the azure.
The sullen darkness remains as common as money
And as fleeting as death.

"But what about you? Yes, you! Didn't you also worship
The scission, the seething, instead of the monument?
Searching for an epitaph in every motet?
Wringing an emblem out of every injury?
Didn't you see your dented ego in every cappuccino?

—"It's true. Upright yet, I dream of the literal.
Sure. Until the end, those embarrassments, radishes,
Paradises, roses, embellishments, tired comparisons. Up
To this sheet of paper, these corpses of letters."

Adieu the poets write their whole lives long
And greying like lavender in November
They hang around, gangrene and gags and riddles,
Pathetically begging for mercy,
Like me for the wear on these eyes and ears
That loved you, that love you.

Ten Ways of Looking at P.B. Shelley

I

His body washed up on the beach
and lay there while the gold drained away
behind the mountains.
In his yellow trousers, in his white silk socks,
in Keats's poems in his inside pocket,
the only moving things were worms.
O wild west wind,
breath of autumn's being.

2

His face had been eaten away
by the creatures of the sea.
His spirit, which had eyes,
lips and nostrils,
saw the dreaming earth
and licked her,
breathing in the smells that destroy
and preserve at once.

3

All skin and bones, spastic.
(In pantomimes he always
played the witch.)
A shrill voice. A magpie's eyes.
Girls at his knee.
And him just squawking
about angels of rain,
angels of lightning
that would come down tonight
on the blue planet.

4

He hated minced pork,
saints, devotion, the King.
But most of all he hated
one man and one woman
and their monogamous embrace.

Black rain, fiery hail
beat down on the fluttering locks
of the maenad wig
he'd put on.

5

There were many thorns, many bushes
into which he fell and bled.
But he always carried arsenic,
because who knows
if you will want to survive
the beauty of inflections?
Who knows if you wouldn't rather
sink with no farewells
into the seaweed, untamed?

6

He once set fire to Mr. Laker,
the family butler. In Italy
he danced by the flames of a forest fire.
Later, in the shadow, grey
cold, after hours like icicles,
he whispered, "Hear, O hear,
the boughs of heaven and ocean,
tangled in each other."

7

He ran screeching from his room,
he had seen, O, the fat women of Sussex
with eyes where the nipples should be.
Whereas usually in his wintry bed,
he saw a naked babe
rising from a purple sea.

O, lift me as a wave,
a leaf, a cloud.

8

For breakfast and lunch he ate bonbons.
Constipated from the laudanum.
Kidneys and bladder damaged.

His accents and rhythms
blow over the frozen earth.
Echoes of gods and blackbirds
and blasphemies.

9

He refused to wear woollen socks.
Butter made him gag.
Into Harriet, Mary, Clare and the rest,
he inserted a wine-soaked sponge
to prevent pregnancy.

On the edge of many circles
he wanted to banish himself.
He sank in his grand gestures,
the refusals.

10

When his fragments died,
he was interred as an ode and a pamphlet.
The Courier wrote: The infidel has drowned;
now he knows if there is a god or no.

He bounced the bawd of euphony
on his knee.
His heathenism, a remedy
when winter comes
on the west wind.

Lumumba

You gave the wet nurse a shock when you were born
by not crying,
a sign of a good conscience.

You studied at Louvain, a pale bastion.
They taught you *L'Union fait la force*.
Up on his cross the God of the Albinos
said his love knows no bounds
not even in the distant technicolor tropics.

Four-eyed thief and dreamer. Your name became
an insult in Belgian soccer stadiums.
You didn't want to be the son of your forefathers,
not the Eldest, and not the Founder,
they never forgave you that.
The tribes sold you to Mobutu
for a telephone connection,
a license plate, a bank account.
The middlemen stepped in the mud
on your nameless cadaver.

The God of the Albinos has sat down
on your dead body as if on a toilet.

Italo Calvino

On the boat to America, after a late breakfast,
he would sit on the side of the swimming pool
and flirt. A different woman every day,
a journalist, a photo model, a housewife.
We, the other four writers, thought it grotesque.
We were just jealous.

He had the eyelashes of a girl,
the centuries-old scowl of Italian scepticism.
He looked after his complexion, his fingernails, his shoes.

For weeks we crossed the New Continent.
Days in the hot car, with the five of us.
He generally wanted to be behind the wheel, he drove too fast,
swerving too much because he was short-sighted
and too vain to wear his glasses.

He didn't want to drive in the desert.
Holding forth on structure and concept,
on ultimate finiteness from the back seat
until he fell asleep mumbling dipping rhymes.

It is thirty years ago.
We wrote poetry back then without punctuation.
He had lived in the mountains with the partisans,
that makes you mistrust spontaneity.
He found the framework in most phonemes,
praising the skeleton in words and in women.

"Italo, for God's sake put on your glasses!"

"Vivere non basta, caro."

The tumour had already nestled in under his elegant cranium.

Brother

"It's hard," he said, "bloody hard.
And unfair too. I'm finally losing weight."

Autumn outside, a corn field stretching to the end of the road,
the words slip out, the end of the road.
He doesn't say another word.

A plastic tube snakes down his throat.
He hiccups for hours. Can't swallow.

Movement still in his right hand,
which carries the left like a fat lily.
The hand gives me a thumbs-up,
sending signals until his final collapse.

His skin has gone white, childlike.
He squeezes my frightened hand.

I still search for a similarity—ours,
her restlessness,
his impatience (no time for time),
the mistrust and gullibility of both—
and land in our first past,
the one with a world like a meadow with frogs,
like a ditch with eels,
and later, bets and dares, table tennis,
house rules, the 52 cards,
the three dice
and constant unbridled hunger.
(I grow old instead of you.
I eat pheasant and smell the woods.)

His housing is restricted now.
The machine breathes for him,
sucking up the phlegm.
A rattle from his diaphragm
and then his last movement, a sluggish wink.

The migration of a soul. A disposition. A portion cut off.
His body still shrinking
and then suddenly in the face that was dead,
a frown and a cramp
and then a gaping look of fury,
unbearably lucid, the anger and terror
of a tyrant. What does he see? Me, a man
turning away in cowardly surprise at his tears?
Then morning comes and they undo the straps.
And he is forever

from **Cruel Happiness** [1999]

What to Speak About

What to speak about tonight? Speaking
in a country we recognise, tolerate,
seldom forget.
This country with its slapstick genesis,
its clammy climate, its filthy stories
about the old days,
its inhabitants, grasping until they finally collapse
between the cauliflowers.
They keep on multiplying
in a paradise of their own invention,
craving happiness, trembling, mush in their mouths.
Like in nature,
where our runts of hills are depilated,
our fields scorched, our air poisoned,
yet the unsuspecting cows keep grazing.

Speaking about this country's writing,
publications full of question marks
on patient paper
continually shocked by its history
and fleeing into deceptive shorthand.
Speaking about the heavy drapes
people draw around themselves.
But we hear them still, the stinking
primates who corner each other in rooms.
Like in nature,
where the hibiscus gives off no scent,
leaving that to the innocent cows who sink
into the drenched earth.

Speaking in this country of gleaming grass,
in which man,
that immoderate worm, that dreaming carcass,
lingers among the cadavers which, dead as they may be,
remain obedient to our memories.
Like our nature which expects a single, solitary
miracle that will eventually, finally
illuminate what one was,
not just this shabby spectacle
thrown together by time.

Speaking about time, which, so they say,
will remain like a brand and a palimpsest?
We lived in an age of using
and being useful.
What defence can we offer for that?
Which festive feathers in our caps?
Which song in the cellar? Maybe.
Say it. Maybe.
A few scratches on slate
to mark the silhouette of your lover.
Fingerprints in clay for her hips.
Phonemes of delight that sometimes resounded
as she, when she, cried out for you like a cat.

Speaking about her presence
wakens the violet hour of twilight.
Like in nature,
the merciless, glassy azure
of our planet seen from Apollo.
And even if your party hat begins
to weigh heavily from speech alone
and the lifeline on your palm

begins to fester,
still, nonetheless, in spite of this
honour the flowering
of the shades that inhabit us,
the shades that beg for comfort.
And stroke her shoulder blade.
Like a hunchback's hump.
Still craving a cruel kind of happiness.

Interview

There's a knocking on my door
and, yes, it's the young poet
—I recognise his teeth—
who once sang the glory of my alliteration
and—oh, familiarity!—has gnawed
at my ankles in the papers ever since.

I bid him enter.

He says he lives from readings
and interviews for magazines.
His wife has been depressive since her teens.

I help him out of his coat.
I pour him a shot of jenever.

His letting me have it in the paper, he says,
was hard, a bitter cup, and not his intent.
It was forced on him by the editor of the cultural supplement.
Our talk would be, broadly speaking,
not too long, about love without stains,
and politics, without naming any names.

I pour him another drink.

"Between you and me," he says, "I find you at odds
with the new,
not recognising the spirit of the age and
venerating dead masters far too much.
Where in your work is the exhilaration of technology?

Because if technology is our divinity and our destiny
shouldn't we join together to reflect
on the laws of the Internet?"

Another jenever. With a beer chaser.
"And excuse me for saying so but
you're sometimes very hermetic."

> Hermetic? Me? In my old age,
> with my laughter tamed,
> and my thunder all in vain?
> Who sits here quivering,
> copying the existing
> all the same.

"And your rhyming patterns are so obvious,
so childishly obvious.
Rhyme doesn't do a thing for *me*.
And apropos of that, what's actually
the underlying concept in your flossofy?
You don't leave me any the wiser."

> I think of an earlier life.
> The rams' heads clashed.
> The rabbits all had names.
> The turkeys gobbled for grain.
> I shouldered my air rifle to shoot
> the guinea fowl in their granny's aprons.
> I think of faraway countries.
> The spectral moon rat that stays alive
> because of its stench.
> The lamp-eyed lemurs.
> The orang pendek that steals children

and loves human liver.
I think of the dead masters.
Byron who kept and numbered
locks of his own hair. His manuscripts.
Lots of crossing out. Lots of second thoughts
but he always left the rhymes intact.
Ezra Pound in the cinema screaming
with laughter at idiotic comedies.
His Ezivursity.
How he kept silent for years and years
then said, "I did it all wrong."
Stevie Smith who thought that everything
could swim in a wonderful wisdom.
"Stepping stones," I say.

"Pardon?" he says.

"Stepping stones the poem can follow.
Gezelle and Minne
have led the way."
And I help him into his coat.
And I lead him to the door.

Outside I point up at the moon.
He keeps staring at my finger.

from In Case of Emergency [2004]

Horizon

The horizon is the language, the language I am
expected to share
with the mutilated child,
the youth who's become a soldier,
so proud of his boots,
the greybeard with his ripped bowels
in his arms.

It rains phosphorus and sirens.

The voices of my country,
mostly in the television.
Murderous families.
A criminal chorus.

And the blood-slurping gods all around.

Our Century

(for Pierre Alechinsky)

In my youth: smudges, curls
gouges
After my youth: coloured shadows
rusted, scorched
something like a past
written down, photocopied, enlarged
primary colours
—the reeds disobedient—
soot
hay
prickly or smothered in asphalt

Since my youth: salt and wind
Splinters in distant boats
It's our century
It remains our youth
No better way to
waste it
than surrounded by fingers of grass,
lightning bolts in snow-covered
gardens

Norm

No other expectation—
No assault
No shadow of an offence
The revulsion resounds
up to the last
desecrated song

Imbalance as the norm
Swimming or flying
In nature
with its splotches and rags

Rehearsal

I wish I was dead.
Like forty-five per cent
of Belgians

I have no one
"Because you never invested
in love, sweetie"

I begin
Continue
Sodium thiopental
There, you're almost unconscious
Then pancuronium bromide
Your lungs fail
Then potassium chloride
And your heart stops

I'll never remember all that

Eris

There is sorrow's rubbish
art's obscene charter
always somewhere always elsewhere.

There is Eris who wanders
on blood-stained feet
searching the thirsty grass
for the bodies of my friends.

When you see her it's too late.
Die while you, like always,
are saying your hellos.

For Hugo

CEES NOOTEBOOM

An Address Delivered Beside his Coffin at the Farewell Ceremony
Bourla Theatre, Antwerp, 29 March 2008

"Des chênes qu'on abat," said Malraux on De Gaulle's death. He was like an oak that has been felled. Suddenly there's an opening in the forest, a place where light can penetrate and feed new growth. But first there's a long period of nothing, a large hole, with weirdly shaped roots perhaps, raised up and clawing at the light, as if searching for life. We're all familiar with such places. Walking through a dark forest, you suddenly come across a strip of clear, filtered light. You can still recall the shape of the enormous tree that stood there, you feel the forest's phantom pain and your own—something that has always existed is gone. Many friends must have experienced it the same way. Hugo as one of the dead, that was new to us. We'd known him in so many guises and in so many settings, but dead, no, not that. It's hard to get used to. We still find it difficult to believe. We hear his name constantly around us, in private conversations and broadcast on radio programs and TV talk shows. If there was a platonic listening post floating through space somewhere, it would be continually picking up those sounds, the U, the O, the AU. Hugo Claus. And if we think of all those voices together, making those sounds at the same time, we hear a deafening hurricane with the vowels and consonants of his name, a high-pitched whistling and a gale-force growl, something that takes your breath away, just as those who knew in advance of the day and the hour last week could not breathe on that day and at that hour.

And now? It's still confusing. That bright spot in the forest, the place where the tree that should have been allowed to stand forever has disappeared, fills slowly with images—fleeting and clear, melancholy and cheerful. Hugo bowing awkwardly at his umpteenth premiere, Hugo with his voice from the old days reading "Even Now" in an auditorium deep in the provinces, Hugo impatient and restless in a museum in Basel or Venice, but you *know* that he sees more than you, Hugo asleep next to you in the cinema, Hugo lazing on the couch while on TV the one hundred riders of the Tour de France work themselves into a lather racing up the Tourmalet. Followed by that other Hugo, the Hugo of the last years, the last weeks. Fragile, alert. It was like he was walking on mirrors, and because of that it was partly as if we had to learn how to walk again as well. Because how do you walk in the presence of death? How do you obey the unspoken commandment to avoid sentimentality, the question that is not allowed to be spoken out loud, how do you act at a court you are visiting for the first time, where an invisible guest we haven't met before joins us at the table, our friend's new friend, with whom he has a prior engagement? Had someone written our roles without writing them down? And had they made it so that it was impossible for us to act because everything was uncompromisingly real in a way that the theatre can never be real? We didn't have any lines, how did we know our lines? Ceremonies of farewell, that I see as a gift he has given me for the time I have left, the clink of glasses, quiet conversations about the world that will retain its validity for a little while yet, laughter and song, and through it all that one unmistakable voice, recognizable always and everywhere, with the accent nobody could pin down because it, like the words he spoke in it, was an emissary from such an individual universe that we, the others, could have an inkling of it, but no more than that. No one could come all too close, his work was both an entrance and a barrier, the almost endless mass of words with the equally endless number of ways of combining them in sonnets or novels, dialogues or quatrains, ghazals, film scripts and deliberately lame haikus, litanies and novellas that rose like a rampart around the inner core of his being, which for me lies concealed in his most beautiful line about himself: "a happy man surprised by doubt."

Over the last few days I re-read two of his novellas, *The Last Bed* and *A Sleepwalk*. The man who could be so light-hearted when playing, who could beam when, with a lethal clang from a distant position, he neutralized the metal ball you had positioned so dangerously in a game of pétanque, who could tell obscene stories about actresses with the verve of a Venetian courtier and laugh when revealing the trump he'd saved for the last trick, displays in *The Last Bed* a dark universe of victims and punishment, of fear, suppressed lust and bloody violence, of mankind's abject pettiness and cruelty, a satanic vision that ends with destruction and death, in which, like Dante, the poet leads you around a layer of hell. Something else is happening in *A Sleepwalk*, a book like a prophesy, in which the writing gives you an insight into the landscape he saw before him in 2000, a horror of forgotten faces, former loves, a guessing game of words lost in each other. And once more he demonstrates his mastery, because showing the drama of broken tools requires brilliant and subtle control over words and sentences. Knowing that you are describing your own fate, you must dare to penetrate deep into the territory of your future misery and humiliation to write for yourself and others about the tragedy that awaits you. And so you say eclipses instead of ellipsis, you no longer know that the woman standing before you was once the woman you wanted above all else, you describe the battlefield and tell yourself that you will leave it before the last weapon has been knocked out of your hands, and then you live on for seven years like a king in his final days, say goodbye to your wife and friends and do what you had resolved to do, knowing that the small-minded want to drag you back to this earthly hell, claiming that enduring it will earn you heavenly paradise. You turned that eternal lie on its head as only you could.

The first time I saw you, you were young and I was even younger, the last time you were old, but the youth you had been still shone through the old master, his smile and mischief were still intact. Today, sad and celebrating, I say goodbye to those two men and all the other men in between. Dear friend, fare well. I only ask one thing: make sure to haunt us.

Translator's Acknowledgments

The selection and translation of these poems was an enjoyable but daunting task and I am very grateful for the generous help provided by a number of people who have built up their knowledge of Claus and his poetry over years, if not decades, of specialization and study. I owe a particular debt of gratitude to Georges Wildemeersch and Dirk van de Geest for making space in their busy schedules and would also like to thank Victor Schiferli and Patrick Peeters for their time and advice, Tom van de Voorde for his encouragement and for reading a draft of the translation and comparing it to the original, and P.C. Evans and Rokus Hofstede for help with particular poems.

I selected the poems from the almost 1,500 pages of Claus's two-volume collected poems and tried to choose representative works from all periods of his extremely diverse poetic oeuvre, not limiting myself to his most famous poems, but also including examples of his latter work, poems from the erotic series *Morning, You* (first published as loose pink cards in a purple velvet box) and Knittelvers from *Almanac*.

While researching the work, I read, browsed and consulted quite a lot of secondary literature, most importantly books and essays by Paul Claes, Dirk de Geest and Georges Wildemeersch and articles and essays by J.M. Coetzee, Bart Eeckhout, Frank Lekens, Kristel Markoen and Patrick Peeters. I also referred to many existing translations, specifically French translations by Marnix Vincent and Maddy Buysse, Franco Paris's Italian translation, Maria Csollány's German, and English translations by J.M. Coetzee, John Irons, Peter Brown & Peter Nijmeijer, and Paul Claes, Christine D'haen, Theo Hermans & Yann Lovelock. My fellow translators' interpretations and solutions often helped me to discover new depths in the original poems and find new possibilities for my own translations. Similarities between my translations and the existing English translations are inevitable, not just because the best translation of a word or phrase is sometimes the most obvious one, but also because Claus sometimes refers back to English sources in direct and indirect quotes.

David Colmer
Amsterdam, Septembert 2013

archipelago books
is a not-for-profit literary press devoted to
promoting cross-cultural exchange through innovative
classic and contemporary international literature
www.archipelagobooks.org